FIRST EDITION

Sixth Printing

Published in the United States of America
By Eakin Press, P.O. Box 23066, Austin, Texas 7873'

ISBN 0-89015-259-4

To our parents
and to our ancestors
who made it possible for us to live in Texas

FOREWORD

In the fall of 1978, my husband, Jerry, made the original suggestion that we "go outhouse hunting" for the purpose of making photographs of these rapidly disappearing structures. I met his suggestion with some reluctance but I was intrigued by the idea of what we might find.

I certainly was not prepared for the variety of outbuildings waiting for us or for the warm-hearted, friendly Texans that would greet us.

The survival of outhouses near historic homes or buildings is an example of the frugal spirit of earlier Texans. On a jaunt to Jefferson, Texas, we were disappointed to find that privies did not accompany the beautiful historic homes that grace the area. In contrast, the predominately German towns of Independence, Brenham, New Ulm, and Industry presented a wide assortment of little johnnies.

After we collected about twenty-five photographs, Jerry insisted that I write captions to appear underneath. My immediate response, "What can you say about an outhouse?", was followed by many interviews with senior citizens in nursing homes or senior citizens' centers. Interviews were not limited to elderly people. Information came from anyone, whom I could persuade to talk about the subject.

The friendliness and hospitality of Texans will never be forgotten. Gifts ranged from seeds for unusual flowers for our garden to an old milk of magnesia bottle for my bottle collection. Each story or recollection brings to mind the face of a person. These people provided the material for the text.

Correspondence with the Smithsonian Institute, Center for Southern Folklore, and the archivist for Sears, Roebuck, and Company revealed that there was no printed material available concerning the subject of outdoor toilets. Trips to the public libraries were unrewarding with the exception of one little volume called *Gems of American Architecture,* copyrighted in 1935.

In the spring of 1980, we were forced to retrace our steps to some of the outhouses we had visited previously in order to make color photographs for publicity. (The photographs for the book were done exclusively in black and white.) To our surprise some outhouses had been demolished. This is the purpose of the book: to preserve a part of Texas' past that will soon be nonexistent.

INTRODUCTION

Only a few remnants of pioneer life of Texas remain today. An occasional outdoor toilet or "privy" is one that lingers on the Texas landscape. The Hill Country, West Texas, the Panhandle, East Texas . . . all boast a few surviving privies.

Some are old. Some are new. Some are renovated combinations of old and new. With each there is a tidbit of folklore or information that will soon be forgotten.

The beaten path to the door of an outhouse is a sure sign of its daily use. An aging black woman may testify that only the backhouse is left from the original buildings of the homesite due to the destruction of fire or the passing of time.

Two vacant houses built by the same family stand side by side . . . one new and one old. The old privy remains between the two houses. A visitor can almost feel the heat of a hot summer day and smell the fragrance of honeysuckle on a trip to the lattice framed "little johnnie."

A Victorian mansion may stand with its complimenting outdoor toilet in the rear. Cold winter nights in the old houses with high ceilings made occupants delay trips to the outbuilding and resort to decorated china chambers or enameled slop jars which were emptied the next day.

Insects delighted in haunting visitors to the privy. The sting of the wasp and the bite of the spider are central themes of humorous outhouse tales.

What secrets were shared between giggling young girls behind the closed door of a privy? What grief or problem was kept from others by a retreat to the outhouse?

The shaded rear lawn of old homesites may have a vacant spot where the surviving fig trees once shaded the family outhouse. More than one gem has escaped demolition due to a person dedicated to preserving the old. The surviving outhouses are the remaining architectural fragments of an earlier generation of Texans.

The earliest outhouses were roofed with wood shingles and featured shuttered vents on the sides of the structure. One antique outhouse presents curved, wooden embellishements near the gables of a pitched roof.

Designs on the doors of these remaining relics include diamonds, stars, quarter moons, and circles. Closures for the privy range from the usual metal hook and eye to the crude handcrafted wooden peg and slot closure.

Seating facilities of the early days consisted of rough hand hewn oval shaped holes. People began to update the privy by placing commode seats over the rough holes for added comfort.

Other conveniences of the outhouse were holders designed for storing corn cobs and a special cardboard box for holding the Sears and Roebuck Catalog, the Montgomery Ward Catalog, and the "Comfort Magazine."

Johnnies, Biffies, Outhouses, Etc. strives to capture the privy in its natural Texas and to preserve some of the humor, some of the romance, and some of the facts that surround the few surviving outhouses that are reminiscent of early Texas.

ACKNOWLEDGEMENTS

We would like to express our appreciation to the following people for their assistance in the preparation of this book: Oscar Seward, Evie Wooten, Judy Hickle, Art Hickle, Fletcher Poole, Mildred Poole, Mattie Callendar, Dona Coulter Carnes, Lillie Maude Cook, Albert Cook, Vivian Farris, Annie Elizabeth Cole, Blanche Fannin, K.C. Kyle, Gwen Jones, Madge Wallace, Robert Denman, Doris Denman, Suzy Kuttler, Joe Evans, Dorothy Mallett, Leon Holbert, Anna Kellett, Warren A. Ramsey.

Special thanks to Munson Engineering, Inc., Edward D. Munson, P.E., President, for the blueprint drawings of an outhouse.

"The flies were thick in that corner of the yard."

The location of the outhouse was always behind the house in a far corner. This kept the stench and insects as far away from the house as possible yet close enough for the women and children to use it. In pioneer days the outhouse was reserved for them exclusively.

Fig trees were planted around the outhouse. The trees benefitted from the constant replenishing of the soil and provided a quick shade for the privy.

Trumpet bloomer vines, wisteria, morning glory vines, and coral vine were seen growing around the outhouse. A foyer was created from lattice work or solid boards placed in front of the privy door. Vines were planted to grow on the blind.

Shady, secluded spots were favored. Users wanted a cool place in summer as well as privacy in all seasons.

If the house faced south, the toilet placed in the rear corner of the yard presented its face to the south and welcomed cold north winds from the rear. The privy was sometimes placed beneath the shade of a large tree to provide an anchor for the structure. Tying the outhouse to a tree kept it from being overturned by high winds. Privies were known to be precariously balanced on a ravine with the rear conveniently placed so that wastes fell into the space below.

ONLY a privy like this would be fitting for an elegant Victorian mansion. Complete with its own privacy screens, it features three holes.

THE quarter moon on the door of the privy provided light as well as ventilation. Other symbols appearing on privy doors were stars, diamonds, and hearts.

The crescent moon with its points corresponding to the curve of the right hand index finger and thumb is called the waxing moon. There are many meanings according to ancient folklore. Some authorities say that the crescent moon pointing upward is holding water and forecasts a dry spell.

NEGATIVE aspects of the outhouse were the sting of the wasp and the odor of the atmosphere. Ventilation in the form of shuttered squares in the rear, a pipe on the roof, or a cut out on the door was a must.

OCCASIONALLY people refused to use modern indoor toilet facilities after they acquired them. One man was heard to declare, "I'll go where I have plenty of room!" He continued to frequent the backhouse and left the modern facilities to the other family members.

SOME privies are of historical importance. This one served the home occupied by Margaret Lea Houston and family during the 1830's at Independence, Texas. Square, shuttered ventilators on the back side were a unique feature of this privy.

OTHER names for outhouse included: privy, dry closet, sanitary closet, backhouse, "Mrs. Jones," the library, little Johnnie, biffie, donnicker, jake, outdoor toilet, dooley, and Willie. Some people called them gems of architecture.

LANDSCAPING for the outdoor toilet traditionally included trumpet bloomer vines which ran over the roof and sometimes provided a little shade and privacy.

A TREE provides a resting place for this johnnie. Securing the privy to a tree kept it from falling into the creek below.

A WOOD shingled roof tops this stucco privy. The outhouse was built to match an early Texas stucco home nearby.

THE orientation of the privy depended on the location of the house. The privy was always located behind the house. If the house faced South, the outhouse would be subject to cold north winds from the rear.

''One Halloween we put a privy right in the center of main street.''

Halloween pranks centering around the biffie have existed for generations. A favorite prank was overturning the outdoor toilet. Pranksters soon learned that the age of the toilet determined the degree of strength needed to accomplish the feat. As the waste accumulated at the back of the privy the amount of moisture increased causing the structure to sink. Since privies were built with the weight of the seats on the back, the semi-rotted boards of the lower portion of the chic sale soon became embedded in the moist, fertile ground. Young mischievous boys have been known to abandon the idea after struggling with an ''aged'' outhouse.

Moving the outhouse to a new location was another favorite joke. Outdoor toilets have mysteriously appeared on front lawns, city streets, school yards, and church sites. Overturning the toilet while in use was the highest achievement among privie pranksters. Even fishermen have been surprised by the sudden appearance of a biffie floating down the river.

EARLY schoolhouses often had only one outhouse for both sexes. The use of the privy was accomplished under the watchful eye of the schoolmarm or master. An additional chore of the teacher was to keep the privy doors washed clean of ugly words. A ventilation pipe on the roof is an unusual aspect of this outdoor toilet.

THE owners of this residence tagged their outhouse "the parlor." Perhaps this was a fitting name for the little room always ready to receive visitors.

COTTON fields of the Brazos Bottom present a landscape covered with cotton punctuated by an occasional backhouse.

A ROUTINE chore of pioneer days was cleaning the outhouse. A good housekeeper provided a bucket of lime and a bucket of ashes. An application of lime then ashes kept the stench of the privy to a minimum. The ashes were often labeled "wood ashes" since they were the by-product of the wood-burning fireplace, heater, or stove.

"Our chore on Saturday was to scrub the seats of the backhouse with lye soap."

Cleaning the privy has always been a dreaded chore. In spite of attempts at cleanliness oldtimers recall that the flies were thick in the corner of the yard where the outhouse stood. There was a surviving odor that housekeepers tried to squelch with homemade lye soap.

Definite procedures were followed for maintenance of the little johnnie. First, the seat area had to be scrubbed with lye soap which bleached the boards snowy white. Second, the area beneath the privy hole had to be cleaned. This chore often served as punishment for children who disobeyed their parents. The debris beneath the privy was carted away to be buried or mixed with the topsoil in the garden area.

Daily maintenance included sprinkling lime over the area beneath the privy holes. The bucket of lime and an accompanying tin can to be used as a scoop were kept nearby. Sweeping the privy was part of the woman's household routine as well as stocking it with a good supply of corn cobs or old catalogs. The broom stood in one corner while the "Sears and Roebuck Catalog" hung over the string stretched taunt between two nails. The cobs were kept in a box or in a special box-like holder made to hold them in a vertical position and attached to the wall.

Another source of paper was "The Comfort Magazine," a periodical for women. It featured recipes and fictitious stories for women.

After the appearance of toilet tissue a customer wrote to Sears, Roebuck, and Co. requesting a roll. The company promptly replied asking for the catalog number of the item. The customer's response followed: "If I had the catalog, I wouldn't need the toilet paper!"

City dwellers in the early 1900's enjoyed the services of a scavenger who drove a cart pulled by mules or horses. He haunted the alleys behind the houses as he emptied the privies. A monthly fee guaranteed the scavenger's regular arrival accompanied by the "honey wagon." Failure to pay might result in the "boarding up" of the privy door.

SOME outhouses were elevated on stakes or posts. The area underneath had to be cleaned regularly. A few biffies had trenches at the rear which were covered with lime and dirt periodically.

THE dark hours between 11 p.m. and 5 a.m. provided the setting for scavenger service according to some city rules of the 1900's. Privy boxes were located in the back of the city outhouse. These were removed at least twice weekly.

SCAVENGER service demanded a fee which entitled the owner of a city privy to a license. Failure to pay could result in the ''boarding up'' of the owner's privy.

MANY people remember the "moonlight man" who came at midnight to clean the privy. This was a common practice in cities in the 1920's. Children were often wakened by the sounds of the scavenger filling his "honey bucket."

IN the early 1900's outhouses within cities were inspected regularly by sanitary officers. Scavengers drove "honey wagons" to collect the treasure deposited in a privy box. A privy box was a receptacle placed under the hole of the outhouse and was removed and emptied or replaced periodically. A "honey wagon" was a mule drawn cart equipped with manpower and shovel.

THE visit of the scavenger was often announced by the pungent aroma that surrounded the house on cleaning day. A summer's outing in the porch swing could easily be spoiled by his visit.

. . . THEN there's the story of the father who didn't want his children to go on a scavenger hunt because the scavenger is the man who cleans outhouses.

THE owner of two outhouses used the labels Mrs. Jones and Mrs. Smith. Users might be required to designate which privy they had occupied.

AN unusual aspect of this outhouse is its attachment to the house that it serves. A ventilation pipe to the outside makes the atmosphere more pleasant.

THE homesite of General Sam Houston and family in 1854 at Independence, Texas, features this outhouse which has stood for over seventy years. The floor is of native stone.

THE new and old methods of sanitation may exist side by side. At this church site the modern sani-serve toilet stands beside the little johnny of yesteryear.

PLENTY of ventilation is the main attraction of this outhouse located on a deer lease near Carlos, Texas. A single light bulb provided illumination for occupants.

THE children's hole deserves special attention. It was not often found, but was immortalized in James Whitcomb Riley's poem, "Passing of the Backhouse." Riley penned the famous lines, "I'm now a man, but none the less I'll try the children's hole."

"My grandpa used to cut the tops out of fancy ladies' hats and nail the brims around the privy holes."

The privy hole could be round, oval, or square, small or large, or smooth or rough. Privies presented seating accommodations for one, two, or three, and added to everyday conversation the expressions, "one-holer," "two-holer," and "three-holer."

The small children's hole was designed to meet the needs of children and diminish their fear of "falling in." The pit privy which followed gave many children new fears with its large, deep, pipe extending to depths unknown.

Attempts were made to add comfort to the outhouse by attaching commode seats to the privy holes. This came after the appearance of commodes for indoors. Earlier biffie owners were known to nail hat brims over the holes in an effort to "pretty up" the interior.

An oval hole was never a perfect oval nor was a round hole perfectly round. The carpenter's skills influenced the degree of perfection. The privy seat was made from two boards combined to make the needed width for the holes. Placing oneself on the privy hole required a special skill developed after a few pinches caused by the slight shifting of the boards as the weight of the human body was placed on them.

Some holes were sanded or worn smooth. Others were rough. An occasional seat had a wooden lid made by hinging the piece of wood that had been removed from the seat to make the hole. The hinges were sometimes made of leather nailed to the lid and to the seat.

BUILT in 1865, the Barton House at Salado, Texas, features a "3 holer." The home and outhouse were constructed for the family of Dr. Wilbourn Barton, the first physician in the area.

THE two holer provided an ideal spot for private chats between two people. Mischievous children were known to throw rocks underneath the privy to invade privacy. Another trick was to remove the back cover of the biffie and allow the dogs to go underneath.

CLEVER tricks were often used to ''fancy up'' the outdoor toilet. One scheme was to cut the crown from outdated ladies' hats and tack the brim to the seat of the toilet.

LITTLE girls on a trip to the privy might let a bonnet string slip too far into a ''one holer'' or ''two holer.'' A pioneer mother with a sense of humor might simply snip off the bonnet string!

"HIS" and "Her" outhouses feature burlap coverings over the doorway. These biffies provide the old style straight boards for sitting rather than the conventional oval seats.

THE Saur-Beckmann Farmstead at Lyndon B. Johnson State Park includes an outhouse. The ''living history'' farm is complete with livestock and chores of a farm during the period 1915-1918.

THE chic sale on the premises of the Johnson Settlement, Johnson City, Texas, was built from the remains of a log cabin which stood in the 1850's. The privy compliments the restored log cabin reminiscent of early Texas life.

THE owners of this "little johnny" felt it was the perfect spot for their birdhouse.

"I used to go to the privy to cry."

Outhouses were used for many purposes other than the original outdoor bathroom. It was an ideal spot for meditation. The chic sale was a little warm in summer, but a conclusion to a problem could be reached quickly when prompted by heat, odor, and the buzzing of a fly, dirt dauber, or wasp.

Sharing secrets in the privacy of the biffie was special for giddy young girls revealing the details of a first romance. Little brother or sister lurked outside hoping to hear a portion of the conversation.

The chic sale could be used for storage. Owners have been known to hang riding gear on the inside. The slop jar was displayed here after it had been cleaned. Nails were driven into the walls on either side of the seats to be used for hanging these items.

The privy was a favorite hiding place. Women who wanted to avoid washing dishes often escaped to the outdoor toilet. Children wanting to avoid punishment or chores found refuge here.

TWIN outhouses are located on the site of the Baptist Church at Independence, Texas, where Sam Houston and his family worshipped. The church was established in 1839.

"EARMARKS" of age for these outhouses are overlapping wood shingles on the roof and the square, shuttered ventilators on the end of each outhouse.

A PAVILION for field workers at Flat, Texas, presents clearly designated areas for MEN and WOMEN.

THE perfect spot for a hammock is beside this abandoned chic sale.

A COMMUNITY privy located behind commercial businesses was used in early days.

"Men and boys went to the barn . . ."

Pioneer settlers of Texas did not have the luxury of an outhouse. The very first sanitation methods required trips to the barn for everyone. A board was placed at a diagonal position in the corner of the fence. The user simply rested his legs on the board.

This was followed by the shield. A large piece of tin nailed to two posts embedded in the ground provided a shield for private moments. After the shield, the privy with no roof appeared. This was more luxurious than the shield but gave the occupant the benefit of the elements. The privy seat and walls were there, but economy demanded that the roof be omitted. The lumber and labor required for it could be used elsewhere.

Privies with roofs became the standard followed by more elaborate designs dictated by the wealth of the owner. The next drastic change in the outhouse was the pit privy featuring a large pipe beneath the hole for collecting wastes. The pipe extended into the ground and received chemicals for destroying wastes.

After the privy became a less popular mode of sanitation with the appearance of indoor plumbing, the outdoor toilet acquired an image associated with humor. The mention of the outhouse painted mental pictures of crescent moons on biffie doors occupied by Ozark mountaineers smoking corn-cob pipes.

Many backhouses were destroyed. A few were left to be used in emergencies. Some have been built in rural areas for novelty or to serve a recreational retreat. The remaining examples of the privy are a mixture of new and old that provide a description of the mode of sanitation that preceded indoor plumbing.

IN the earliest days, outhouses were reserved for women and children exclusively. Men and boys balanced themselves on a board placed "katty-cornered" across the barn fence.

ABANDONED privies are often put to other uses. Black-eyed Susans surround this old outhouse flanked by two little sheds.

THE new and the old stand side by side under the spreading old oaks on top of a hill near Industry, Texas.

THE pit privy came after the first outdoor toilets and was often found near railroads or other public buildings. It featured a concrete receptacle or pipe fitted into the ground. Chemicals could be added for sanitation purposes.

The large open pipe extending to depths unknown looked dark and deep to small children making a visit. Recollections include the fear of "falling in."

Employees of the Works Progress Administration supervised the construction of pit privies during the hard times of the Great Depression.

THE necessary Sears and Roebuck Catalog often hung over a string stretched between two nails. The thin black and white pages were favored over the harsher colored pages.

"SEVEN little biffies all in a row" are an added attraction of Lukenbach, Texas. The stone wall in the foreground is just one example of the many uses for the native stone found in the Hill Country.

COUNTRY cemeteries often boast a surviving outhouse. The sagging door tells the age of the outbuilding and serves as a monument to a mode of sanitation that is quickly disappearing.

INSCRIBED on the walls of this jake were these words: August 4, 1921—Kilroy was here.

THE privy of three gables would be an appropriate name for this structure found at New Ulm, Texas. The interior featured two separate rooms with two holes per room. The exterior has delicate curves on either side of the gables and narrow, shuttered vents on the ends.

''The most unusual outhouse I ever saw had a gabled roof with little curlicue shapes under the gables.''

Construction of early privies was done according to the ideas of the carpenter. He relied heavily on memory recalling the outhouses that he had seen.

The most common outhouse made a square about four feet in dimension. The roof was at a slant with the higher point above the front door. Pioneers made a board roof of hand made shingles split from blocks. A primitive tool called the froe was used. The walls of the outdoor toilet were made of rough lumber, tin, native stone, or any material plentiful in supply. Architectural details of outhouses ranged from fancy roof designs to unusual symbols on the outhouse door.

The symbols on the door served as decoration and furnished light and ventilation. Owners requested hearts, diamonds, stars, round openings, or any other shape that pleased the imagination. The quarter moon was a favorite shape for the ventilation hole.

The door could be fastened in many ways. One of the most common methods was a small rectangular piece of wood with a nail driven through the wooden bar and the door with enough space between to allow the bar to rotate. This works well from the outside, but presented a problem for the occupant. Sitting on the privy seat and holding the door at the same time could be difficult. A string was hung on the inside of the door for this purpose. In later years thoughtful builders sometimes provided a metal hook and eye latch for the interior. Early builders seemed to be more concerned with exterior closures.

Another type of fastener was a sliding piece of wood that rested against the door and extended across the opening edge of the door. The wooden piece was supported by two wooden rests, one on either side.

Fancy privies with gables usually complimented more elaborate homes. Owners of Victorian homes liked to paint the outhouse and trim it with lattice work panels to provide a privacy shield in front of the door.

The back of the outhouse where wastes were removed was an open space admitting cold air in winter and flies in summer. Some outhouses had a hinged flap that could be raised and lowered at cleaning time.

A MAJOR disadvantage of the outdoor toilet was the loss of privacy when the latch on the door became disengaged. A favorite joke for boys was to bar the door from the outside when occupants remained inside longer than usual.

STONE privies provided a cool retreat. These are seen in areas of Texas where stone is plentiful.

THE carpenter building a privy must rely on previous experience and a keen memory as guides. Precise plans for outhouses just aren't available. An occasional new one complete with wind chimes and hanging basket may be found.

AT one time this outhouse stood at the railroad depot, Millican, Texas. During the days of the War Between the States a large storage depot was located at Millican.

AVOIDING work could be accomplished with the excuse, "I need to go!" The ideal time for a trek to the outhouse was when dishes needed washing or drying.

A SMALL space at the front of the outhouse door was often hidden from view by a wall or lattice work frame. This area was called "the foyer" and was the setting for schoolyard fights or an illicit smoke. Early schoolhouses had a privy for each sex. If the building did not have a privy, the girls were required to use the bushes in front of the school and the boys were confined to the bushes at the rear of the building. If students could gain permission to go in "twos," secrets were shared.

AN appropriate name for this backhouse appears on the front door. Screen wire at the top of the door furnishes ventilation.

MOONLIGHT travelers might see a light in the outhouses that dotted the country landscape. Lanterns provided light for after dark trips to see "Mrs. Jones." The light could be from a fire made in a bucket with chips and paper. "Fire in a bucket" was used for warmth on cold winter nights. An observer unfamiliar with this practice might think the outhouse was ablaze.

''Sitting on a slop jar on a cold night was rough. We'd sit down real slow waiting to feel the cold rim of the jar.''

Cold weather and convenience demanded the appearance of the chamber. The chamber was a covered pot made of fine porcelain china decorated with delicate patterns. These were confined to the bedroom and kept behind a decorated screen made of silk fabric stretched over a folding frame.

During the days of slavery chambers were used in the upper levels of the large plantation homes. Slaves stood beneath the lower windows waiting for the wastes to be lowered to them in buckets. The buckets were carried to the outlying backhouses to be emptied.

The chamber was followed by the slop jar. The slop jar was an enameled covered container with a handle. The term ''slop'' applied to jar indicated its original use was for slop—a mixture of dishwater, uneaten food, and vegetable peelings fed to thc hogs. This little enamelware container was kept under the bed. It was used during cold winter nights or any other time when trips to the outdoor johnny were not possible.

Emptying the slop jar was a chore for the next day. The container and lid were washed thoroughly and placed in the sun to dry.

OUTHOUSE doors and walls provided a permanent record of the literary achievements of family members. Inscriptions ranged from "Home Sweet Home" on the outside to obscene words on the inside.

MOONLIGHT trips to the privy might lead to an encounter with a mean old gander. This often required matching wits with the old goose in order to return to the safety of the house.

TEACHERS often sent an older boy on a scouting expedition to the outhouse. His main duty was to check the outbuilding for wasps and spiders before the younger children were allowed to go for a visit. The atmosphere of the outhouse provided a haven for spiders, flies, wasps, and dirt daubers.

IN the days of the Old South, human wastes were deposited in chambers. Chambers were covered china containers kept behind the decorative screen in the bedroom. The contents of the chamber was emptied into a bucket, lowered from the windows of the house, and emptied by slaves into the outdoor privy. A unique detail of this outhouse is a round glass window on the side.

YARD chickens often roamed the area near the outhouse. A fastidious homemaker always selected a hen from the bunch to be penned and fattened before killing for the table.

THE year of construction of this outhouse was about 1908. Although it is no longer in use, the owner's reluctance to destroy it is typical of the spirit of economy which marks many descendants of early Texas families.

THE privy provided an ideal hiding place for the pioneer woman who wanted to avoid a persistent traveling peddler. The beaten path suggests frequent use.

"I'll never forget the day . . ."

Every old timer has a favorite story to tell about an embarassing moment relating to the biffie. Victims of rocking or overturning the privy suffered ridicule. Spider bites on private places rank high on the list of amusing tales.

Occupants could be surprised by a smart pony who learned to open the door of the outhouse. Accidental opening of the privy door might reveal a person in a most private moment. The best stance for occupying the privy hole included one hand on the door.

Chickens and dogs were known to enter the privy from behind, peek through the holes of the seat, and enter the outhouse to surprise the person inside the chic sale. This explains the hen's nest often found in the paper box.

The old traveling peddler was known to follow housewives to the door of the privy and demand that they relinquish their hiding place and purchase his wares.

People were sometimes trapped inside the privy by someone holding the door or by a super efficient latch that managed to fall into place on the exterior of the door. Little boys were known to remain hidden until the enemy entered the privy then quietly slip the latch into place or hold the door. This was the ultimate revenge!

People were shy about making a trip to the privy. A common practice was to admit performing a task such as "slopping the hogs and feeding the chickens" then visit the privy on the way back to the house.

WEST Texas storms have been known to trap people inside the outhouse. Trees blown by high winds against the door of a privy could quickly capture the occupant.

A VISIT to Mrs. Jones could be risky. Once a young couple was surprised by a charging bull. The biffie toppled over with them inside.

EVEN ponies learned to open outhouse doors! At least one smart pony belonging to a farm family learned to open the simple wooden latch by pushing the peg out of the slot with his nose. He surprised many visitors!

ONE old timer didn't want to discuss privies. He recalled the punishment that he almost received after pushing an outhouse into the river with an eighty year old man inside.

HENS around the outhouse caused many problems. A favorite spot for a nest was in the rear corner of the privy beneath the toilet seats. Hens would enter the privy through the toilet holes and make a nest in the box where the catalog was kept.

THE outhouse was once used as a prison by a little boy who became angry at the elderly visiting preacher. The little boy waited until he saw the minister enter the privy then barricaded the door and refused to let the old man leave. The preacher refused to remain for an overnight visit.

THE story goes . . . that an old man retired to the privy for a daily visit. He was surprised by a bite from a black widow spider. The visit prompted a trip to the doctor and a few days of recuperation.

ONE oldtimer remembers when a group of devilish youngsters placed a little johnny in the middle of a city street and opened the doors.

ROCKING the outhouse was a favorite sport for energetic young boys. The unlucky person caught inside received quite a shock.

IN early pioneer days young boys delighted in overturning the schoolhouse privy. The angry school trustees threatened to whip each boy in the school unless they revealed the culprit's name. During the 1930's and 1940's, a favorite Halloween prank was turning over the outhouse.

PIONEER children escaped lengthy church services by going to the privy. Smoking behind the privy and writing on the walls were diversions enjoyed there.

ONE descendant of the Lyndon Baines Johnson family recalls the worst ''whippin' of her life'' was her reward for pushing over this outhouse while Aunt Oriole remained inside.

BEING locked in the backhouse could be an uncomfortable situation. One woman tore the door from its hinges in order to get outside. The neighbors heard her screams while family members listened to the full volume of the radio indoors.

IN the rattlesnake country near Gonzales, Texas, women were known to flee the outhouse after sighting one of those poisonous creatures, the snake, coiled beneath the familiar privy hole.

FINDING an outhouse to top the annual bonfire at Texas A & M University is a task for the Corps of Cadets. For them, the outhouse is used to symbolize the Tower located on the campus of their biggest rival, The University of Texas Longhorns. In the early days of the school, the privy was stolen from the local area. In later years, the outhouse has been built by members of the Aggie band and painted orange and white, the colors of the rival school.

PASSING OF THE BACK-HOUSE

When memory keeps me company and moves to smiles or tears,
A weather-beaten object looms through the mist of years,
Behind the house and barn it stood, a half a mile or more,
And hurrying feet a path had made, straight to its swinging door,
Its architecture was a type of simple classic art,
But in the tragedy of life it played a leading part.
And oft, the passing traveler drove slow, and heaved a sigh,
To see the modest hired girl slip out with glances shy.

We had our posy garden that the women loved so well,
I loved it too, but better still I loved the stronger smell
That filled the evening breezes so full of homely cheer,
And told the night-o'ertaken tramp that human life was near.
On lazy August afternoons, it made a little bower
Delightful, where my grandsire sat and whiled away an hour.
For there the summer mornings its very cares entwined,
And berry bushes reddened in the steaming soil behind.

All day fat spiders spun their webs to catch the buzzing flies,
That flitted to and from the house where Ma was baking pies.
And once a swarm of hornets bold, had built a palace there,
And stung my unsuspecting Aunt—I must not tell you where—
Then Father took a flaming pole—that was a happy day—
He nearly burned the building up, but the hornets left to stay.
When summer bloom began to fade and winter to carouse,
We banked the little building with a heap of hemlock boughs.

But when the crust was on the snow and the sullen skies were gray
In sooth, the building was no place where one could wish to stay.
We did our duties promptly, there one purpose swayed the mind,
The torture of that icy seat would make a Spartan sob,
For needs must scrape the gooseflesh with a lacerating cob,
That from a frost-encrusted nail was suspended by a string—
For Father was a frugal man and wasted not a thing.

When Grandpa had to "go out back" and make his morning call,
We'd bundle up the dear old man with a muffler and a shawl,
I knew the hole on which he sat, 'twas padded all around,
And once I dared to sit there—'twas all too wide I found,
My loins were all too little and I jack-knifed there to stay,
They had to come and get me out or I'd have passed away.
Then Father said ambition was a thing that boys should shun,
And I just use the children's hole 'til childhood days were done.

And still I marvel at the craft that cut those holes so true,
The baby hole, and the slender hole that fitted Sister Sue.
That dear old country landmark; I've tramped around a bit,
And in the lap of luxury my lot has been to sit—
But 'ere I die I'll eat the fruit of trees I robbed of yore
Then seek the shanty where my name is carved upon the door,
I ween the old familiar smell will soothe my faded soul,
I'm now a man, but none the less I'll try the children's hole.

JAMES WHITCOMB RILEY

—Photo by Blair L. Fannin

JERRY W. Fannin is an accountant with the Texas Department of Highways and Public Transportation, Bryan, Texas. Photography is a hobby and part time business for him. He specializes in outdoor portraiture concentrating on children.

He is a graduate of Sam Houston University with a degree in business administration.

Jerry and his wife, Angela, are native Texans. Both were born and raised in Madison County and are the parents of a son, Blair Len Fannin.

Angela, the author of the material accompanying the photographs, is also a graduate of Sam Houston University. A former teacher of homemaking, she is a fifth generation Texan and a member of the Daughters of the Republic of Texas and the Daughters of the American Revolution.

Angela's interest in history and Texas lore blends with Jerry's interest in photography to produce this record of part of Texas' disappearing past.

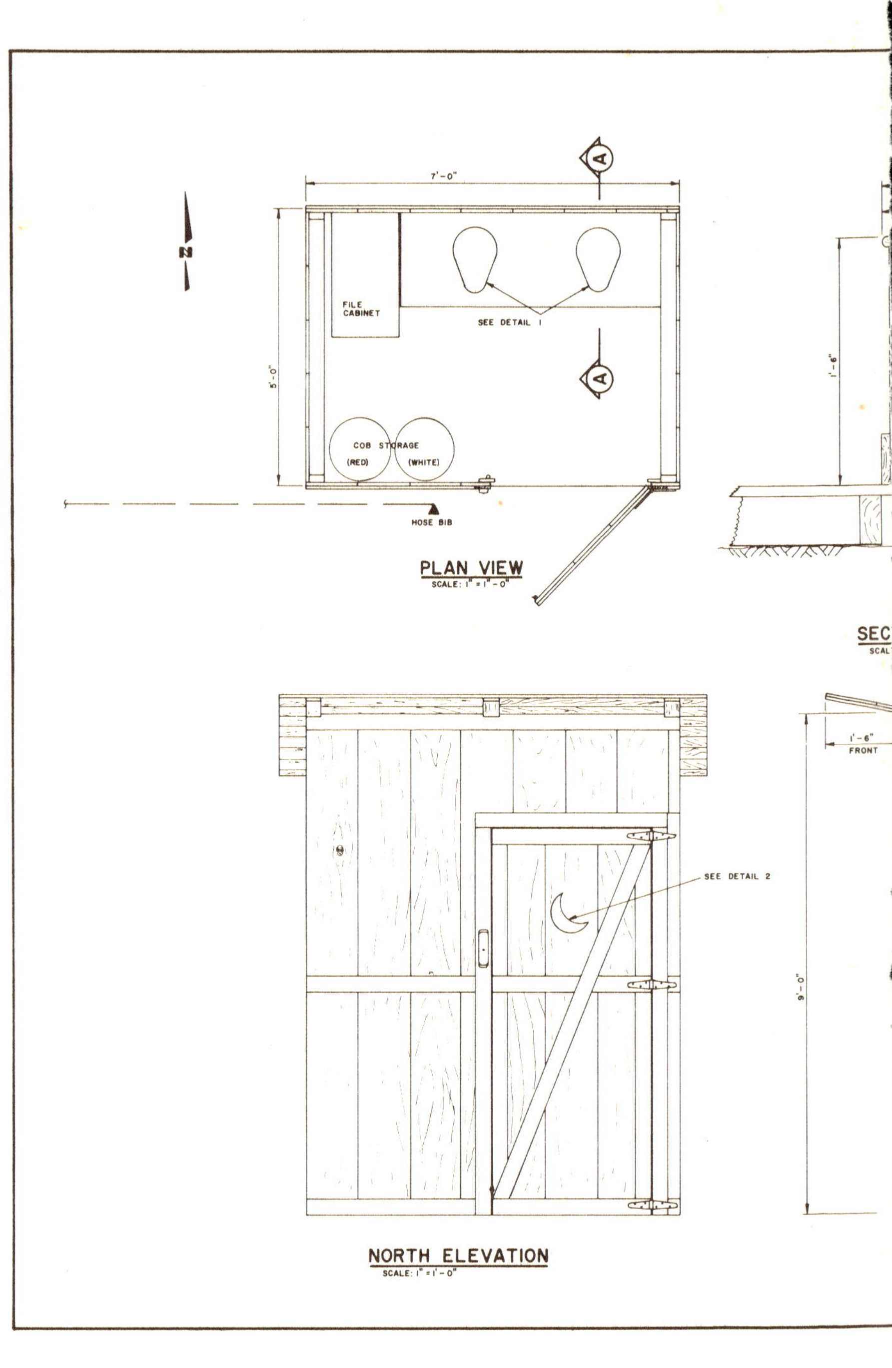

7'-0"
5'-0"
FILE CABINET
SEE DETAIL 1
COB STORAGE
(RED)
(WHITE)
HOSE BIB
A
N
PLAN VIEW
SCALE: 1" = 1'-0"
1'-6"
SEC
SEE DETAIL 2
1'-6"
FRONT
9'-0"
NORTH ELEVATION
SCALE: 1" = 1'-0"